Congressional
Research
Service

Extending Unemployment Compensation Benefits During Recessions

Julie M. Whittaker
Specialist in Income Security

Katelin P. Isaacs
Analyst in Income Security

October 11, 2012

Congressional Research Service

7-5700

www.crs.gov

RL34340

CRS Report for Congress ———————————————

Summary

This report describes the history of temporary federal extensions to unemployment benefits from 1980 to the present. Among these extensions is the Emergency Unemployment Compensation (EUC08) program created by P.L. 110-252 (amended by P.L. 110-449, P.L. 111-5, P.L. 111-92, P.L. 111-118, P.L. 111-144, P.L. 111-157, P.L. 111-205, P.L. 111-312, P.L. 112-78, and P.L. 112-96).

This report contains five sections. The first section provides background information on unemployment compensation (UC) benefits. It also provides a brief summary of UC benefit exhaustion and how exhaustion rates are related to the business cycle.

The second section provides the definition of a recession as well as the determination process for declaring a recession. It also provides information on the timing of all recessions since 1980.

The third section summarizes the legislative history of federal extensions of unemployment benefits. It includes information on the permanently authorized extended benefit (EB) program as well as information on temporary unemployment benefit extensions. It also includes a brief discussion on the role of extended unemployment benefits as part of an economic stimulus package.

The fourth section provides figures examining the timing of recessions and statistics that may be considered for determining extending unemployment benefits.

The fifth section briefly discusses previous methods for financing these temporary programs. In particular it attempts to identify provisions in temporary extension legislation that may have led to increases in revenue or decreases in spending related to unemployment benefits.

This report will be updated to reflect new laws extending unemployment benefits.

Contents

Figures

Tables

Appendixes

Contacts

Unemployment Compensation and Exhaustion of Benefits

The cornerstone of an unemployed worker's income support is the joint federal-state Unemployment Compensation (UC)[1] program, which may provide income support through the payment of UC benefits. The underlying framework of the UC system is contained in the Social Security Act. Title III of the act authorizes grants to states for the administration of state UC laws, Title IX authorizes the various components of the federal Unemployment Trust Fund (UTF), and Title XII authorizes advances or loans to insolvent state UC programs. UC is financed by federal taxes under the Federal Unemployment Tax Act (FUTA) and by state payroll taxes under the State Unemployment Tax Acts (SUTA).

The federal government funds federal and state UC program administration, the federal share (50% under permanent law) of Extended Benefit (EB) payments, 100% of the Emergency Unemployment Compensation (EUC08) program, and federal loans to insolvent state UC programs. States fund regular state UC benefits and the state share (50%) of EB payments. The American Recovery and Reinvestment Act of 2009 (P.L. 111-5, as amended) temporarily provides for 100% federal funding of EB through December 31, 2012.

UC Benefits and Duration

Workers who lose their jobs face serious long-term economic implications. In general, they face a substantially reduced probability of full-time employment and an increased probability of part-time employment. Those workers who find new full-time employment on average experience significantly decreased earnings relative to what they earned before they lost employment.

The UC program pays benefits to workers in covered employment who become involuntarily unemployed for economic reasons and meet state-established eligibility rules. The UC program generally does not provide UC benefits to the self-employed, to those who are unable to work, or to those who do not have a recent earnings history. States usually disqualify claimants who lost their jobs because of inability to work or unavailability for work, who voluntarily quit without good cause, who were discharged for job-related misconduct, or who refused suitable work without good cause.

This temporary unemployment insurance benefit is designed to be sufficient to meet an unemployed worker's basic obligations until the worker finds a new position. Generally, benefits are based on wages for covered work over a 12-month period. The entitlement formula varies by state, typically requiring a substantial work history and replacing up to 50% of workers' wages. Generally, the maximum benefit amount is capped (often half of the average wage in the state or less), which lowers the average national replacement rate to 32.5% of the average weekly wage in the last quarter of 2011.

---

[1] For more information on UC, CRS Report RL33362, *Unemployment Insurance: Programs and Benefits*, by Julie M. Whittaker and Katelin P. Isaacs. For information on the most recent temporary federal unemployment benefit extension, see CRS Report R42444, *Emergency Unemployment Compensation (EUC08): Current Status of Benefits*, by Julie M. Whittaker and Katelin P. Isaacs.

Weekly maximums in July 2012 ranged from $133 (Puerto Rico) to $653 (Massachusetts) and, in states that provide dependents' allowances, up to $979 (Massachusetts). In July 2012, the average weekly benefit was $299. Benefits are available for up to 26 weeks in most states (30 weeks in Massachusetts; 28 weeks in Montana; 25 weeks in Arkansas and Illinois; 20 weeks in Michigan, Missouri, and South Carolina; 12-23 weeks in Florida, depending on the state unemployment rate; 14-20 weeks in Georgia, depending on the state unemployment rate). The average regular UC benefit duration in July 2012 was 17.4 weeks, with almost half (48%) of all beneficiaries exhausting their regular benefits. In July 2012, approximately 3.18 million unemployed workers received regular state UC benefits in a given week. In 2011, on average, 27% of all U.S. unemployed workers received regular state unemployment benefits (when all extended unemployment benefits are included that percentage increases to 54%).

Generally, the UC recipiency rate (the ratio of unemployed receiving UC benefits to all unemployed) rises during economic recessions (as workers with strong labor market experience are laid-off) and falls during economic expansions (as new entrants to the labor market begin to comprise a greater proportion of the unemployed).[2]

Monitoring Search, Generosity of Unemployment Benefits, and Disincentives to Find Work

The difficulty in monitoring job search intensity creates the risk the unemployed will abuse a system designed to alleviate the worst financial aspects of job loss. Although most economists would agree that UC benefits create some disincentives to find work quickly, these disincentives are somewhat balanced by a relatively low replacement rate of wages by UC benefits and a recognition that proper allocation of human resources and human capital requires adequate job search time.[3]

The job-search behavior of the unemployed can be influenced by changing the timing, generosity, and duration of UC benefits. Higher benefit levels and easier program requirements for benefits will cause recipients to be less willing to accept jobs and may alleviate some of the social stigma from being unemployed.[4] The availability of benefits may create a disincentive to search for and accept reemployment, increasing unemployment and unemployment duration.[5] Economic research has suggested that this disincentive effect is relatively small and not a particularly large contributor to the high unemployment rates found during economic recessions.[6]

---

[2] The percentage of UC beneficiaries as compared to all unemployed workers is commonly referred to as the "recipiency rate." The exhaustion rate measures the proportion of all UC benefit recipients who exhaust their UC eligibility and do not find a job within that period.

[3] For a recent summary of available research on this topic, see CRS Report R41676, *The Effect of Unemployment Insurance on the Economy and the Labor Market*, by Thomas L. Hungerford.

[4] For a detailed survey of the disincentive effect, see Gary Burtless, "Unemployment Insurance and Labor Supply: A Survey," in W. Lee Hansen and James Byers, eds., *Unemployment Insurance* (Madison: University of Wisconsin Press, 1990).

[5] Congressional Budget Office, "Options for Responding to Short-Term Economic Weakness," January 2008.

[6] For example, Karen Campbell and James Sherk, *Extended Unemployment Insurance – No Economic Stimulus*, Heritage Foundation, Center for Data Analysis Report #08-13, November 18, 2008, find that an increase in potential duration of 20 additional weeks of unemployment benefits leads to a .22 percentage point increase in the unemployment rate. See also, Bruce Meyer, "Unemployment and workers' compensation programmes: rationale, design, labour supply and income support," *Fiscal Studies*, vol. 23, no. 1 (2002), pp. 1-49. See also Rajeev Chetty, "Moral Hazard versus Liquidity and Optimal Unemployment Insurance," *Journal of Public Economy*, vol. 116, no. 2 (continued...)

UC Benefit Exhaustion

The limited duration of UC benefits (generally 26 weeks[7]) will result in some unemployed individuals exhausting their UC benefits before finding work or voluntarily leaving the labor force for other reasons such as retirement, disability, family care, or education. Empirical research suggests that workers who exhaust benefits search at similar or higher levels of intensity as those workers who do find employment before benefit exhaustion.[8] All state programs attempt to identify potential benefit exhaustees through a state specific profiling system. Workers who are identified as likely to become unemployed long-term may be offered intensive employment services.[9]

Figure 1 displays the percentage of UC beneficiaries both as a percentage of all unemployed workers (the "recipiency rate") and as the number of UC benefit exhaustees since 1979. (Please note that **Figure 1** uses different numerical scales for the recipiency rate and for the exhaustion rate. Because the correspondence between the two scales was determined by scaling size rather than by a particular economic correspondence, readers should not place any significance in the two lines crossing each other. The scale for the recipiency rate is located on the left-hand y-axis. The scale for the UC benefit exhaustees is located on the right-hand y-axis.)

The proportion of UC recipients who exhaust their benefits varies according to economic conditions, state benefit duration formulas, and the composition of the labor force. Some evidence suggests that an aging workforce may have increased the proportion of unemployed workers who are long-term unemployed; at the same time, this aging workforce may also have contributed to the decrease in the overall unemployment rate.[10]

(...continued)

(2008), pp. 173-234.

[7] Benefits are available for up to 26 weeks in most states (30 weeks in Massachusetts; 28 weeks in Montana; 25 weeks in Arkansas and Illinois; 20 weeks in Michigan, Missouri, and South Carolina; 12-23 weeks in Florida, depending on the state unemployment rate; 14-20 weeks in Georgia, depending on the state unemployment rate).

[8] Walter Corson and Mark Dynarski, *A Study of Unemployment Insurance Recipients and Exhaustees: Findings from a National Survey*, U.S. Department of Labor Employment and Training Administration, Unemployment Insurance Occasional Paper 90-3, 1990.

[9] These services may include training on job search, job counseling, and funding for educational and skill-enhancing courses.

[10] For details on these trends, see CRS Report RL32757, *Unemployment and Older Workers*, by Julie M. Whittaker.

Figure 1. Economic Recessions, Percentage of Regular UC Beneficiaries to All Unemployed, and UC Benefit Exhaustees, January 1979-July 2012

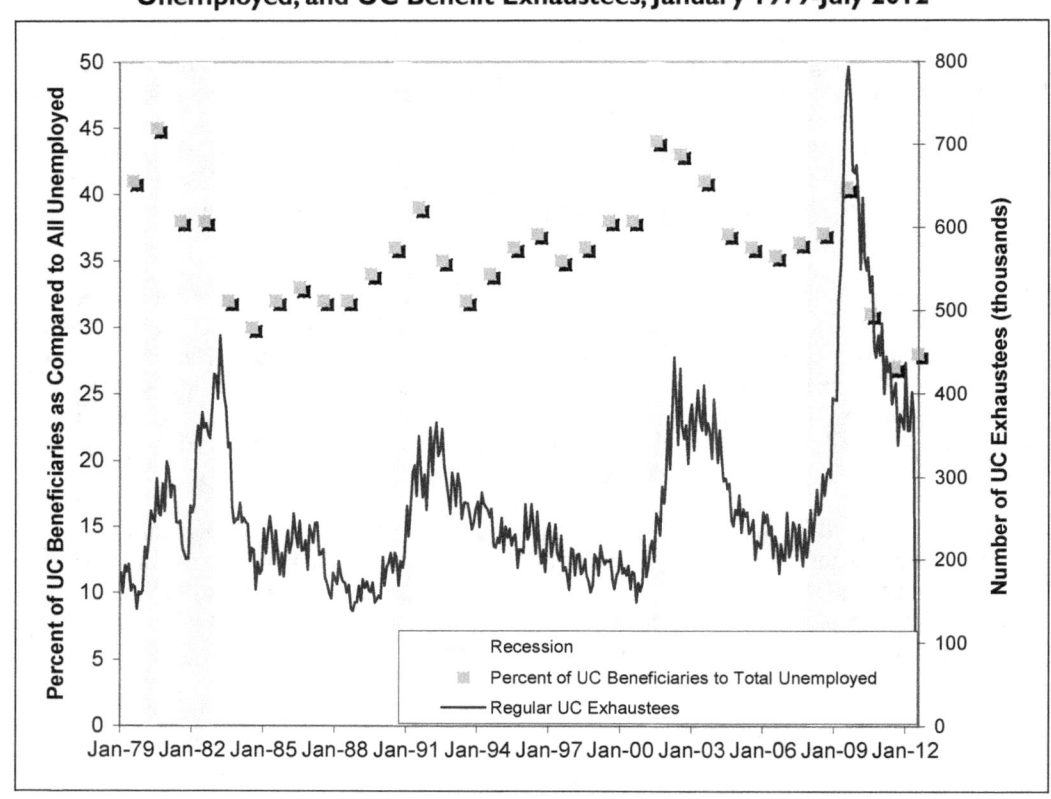

Source: Congressional Research Service. Data are from Department of Labor, Employment and Training Administration. http://www.doleta.gov/unemploy/chartbook.cfm.

Recessions

Determination of a Recession

The National Bureau of Economic Research (NBER)—not the federal government—declares when a recession began.[11] A recession is a significant decline in economic activity spread across the economy, lasting more than a few months, normally visible in measures of real gross domestic product (GDP), real income, employment, industrial production, and wholesale-retail sales.[12] A

---

[11] For a detailed explanation on the determination of recessions, see CRS Report R40052, *What is a Recession and Who Decided When It Started?* , by Brian W. Cashell.

[12] The NBER explicitly states that it considers real GDP to be the single measure that comes closest to capturing what it means by "aggregate economic activity." Therefore, it places considerable weight on real GDP and other output measures. Thus, the NBER takes into account employment but not unemployment or unemployment rates when determining recessionary periods. The NBER's approach is summarized at http://www.nber.org/cycles/recessions.html.

recession begins just after the economy reaches a peak of activity and ends as the economy reaches its trough. Between a trough and a peak, the economy is in an expansion.

Most Recent Recession Began December 2007 and Ended June 2009

The NBER maintains a time line of the U.S. business cycle. This chronology identifies the dates of peaks and troughs that frame economic recessions or expansions. According to NBER, a peak was reached in December 2007, marking the end of the expansion that began in November 2001 and thus marking the beginning of the recession that ended in June 2009.

Recessions from 1980 to Present

Since 1980, there have been five separate periods that the NBER has identified as recessions: January 1980-July 1980; July 1981-November 1982; July 1990-March 1991; March 2001-November 2001; and the December 2007-June 2009 recession.

Federal Programs of Extended Unemployment Compensation

The Unemployment Compensation program's two main objectives are to provide temporary and partial wage replacement to involuntarily unemployed workers and to stabilize the economy during recessions.[13] These objectives are reflected in the current UC program's funding and benefit structure. When the economy grows, UC program revenue rises through increased tax revenues while UC program spending falls as fewer workers are unemployed and receive benefits. The effect of collecting more taxes while decreasing spending on benefits dampens demand in the economy. This also creates a surplus of funds or a "cushion" of available funds for the UC program to draw upon during a recession. In a recession, UC tax revenue falls and UC program spending rises as more workers lose their jobs and receive UC benefits. The increased amount of UC payments to unemployed workers dampens the economic effect of lost earnings by injecting additional funds into the economy.

In response to economic recessions, the federal government sometimes has augmented the regular UC benefit with both permanent (the Extended Benefit program) and temporary extensions (including the Emergency Unemployment Compensation program) of the duration of unemployment benefits.

Extended Benefit Program (Determined at the State Level)

The Extended Benefit (EB) program was established by the Federal-State Extended Unemployment Compensation Act of 1970 (EUCA), P.L. 91-373 (26 U.S.C. 3304, note). EUCA may extend receipt of unemployment benefits (extended benefits) at the state level if certain economic situations exist within the state. The Omnibus Budget Reconciliation Act of 1981, P.L.

---

[13] See, for example, President Franklin Roosevelt's remarks at the signing of the Social Security Act: http://www.ssa.gov/history/fdrstmts.html#signing.

97-35, among other items, amended the EUCA to require that claimants have worked at least 20 weeks of full-time insured employment or the equivalent in insured wages.

The EB program is triggered when a state's insured unemployment rate (IUR)[14] or total unemployment rate (TUR)[15] reaches certain levels. All states must pay up to 13 weeks of EB if the IUR for the previous 13 weeks is at least 5% and is 120% of the average of the rates for the same 13-week period in each of the 2 previous years. There are two other optional thresholds that states may choose. (States may chose one, two, or neither of the additional options.) If the state has chosen the option, they would provide the following:

- Option 1: an additional 13 weeks of benefits if the state's IUR is at least 6%, regardless of previous years' averages.

- Option 2: an additional 13 weeks of benefits if the state's TUR is at least 6.5% and is at least 110% of the state's average TUR for the same 13-weeks in either of the previous two years; an additional 20 weeks of benefits if the TUR is at least 8% and is at least 110% of the state's average TUR for the same 13-weeks in either of the previous two years.

The EB program imposes additional restrictions on individual eligibility for benefits. It requires that a worker be actively searching and available for work. Furthermore, the worker may not receive benefits if the worker refused an offer of suitable work. Finally, claimants must have recorded at least 20 weeks of full-time insured employment or the equivalent in insured wages during their base period (the four quarters of earnings used to determine UC benefit eligibility).

EB Provisions in the American Recovery and Reinvestment Act of 2009

As amended, the American Recovery and Reinvestment Act of 2009 (P.L. 111-5, also known as ARRA or the 2009 stimulus package) contained several provisions affecting unemployment benefits. Among these provisions was a temporary change increasing the federal share to 100% in the cost sharing agreement for EB through December 2011. (The permanent funding arrangement is 50% federal funding and 50% state funding.) ARRA also provided a supplemental $25 weekly benefit through May 2010 for recipients of unemployment benefits, including EB. Finally, ARRA also allows states, at their option, to temporarily change the eligibility requirements for the EB program in order to expand the number of persons eligible for EB benefits.[16]

---

[14] The IUR is the three-month average ratio of persons receiving UC benefits to the number of persons covered by UC. The IUR is substantially different than the total unemployment rate (TUR) because it excludes several important groups: self-employed workers, unpaid family workers, workers in certain not-for-profit organizations, and several other, primarily seasonal, categories of workers. In addition to those unemployed workers whose last jobs were in the excluded employment, the insured unemployed rate excludes the following: those who have exhausted their UC benefits; new entrants or reentrants to the labor force; disqualified workers whose unemployment is considered to have resulted from their own actions rather than from economic conditions; and, eligible unemployed persons who do not file for benefits.

[15] The TUR is a three-month average of the unemployment rate published by the Bureau of Labor Statistics: that is, the ratio of the total number of unemployed persons divided by the total number of employed and unemployed persons.

[16] For additional information, see CRS Report R40368, *Unemployment Insurance Provisions in the American Recovery and Reinvestment Act of 2009*, by Alison M. Shelton and Julie M. Whittaker.

Temporary EB Trigger Modifications in P.L. 111-312

P.L. 111-312 made some temporary, technical changes to certain triggers in the EB program. P.L. 111-312, as amended, allows states to temporarily use lookback calculations based on three years of unemployment rate data (rather than the current lookback of two years of data) as part of their mandatory IUR and optional TUR triggers if states would otherwise trigger off or not be on a period of EB benefits. Using a two-year versus a three-year EB trigger lookback is an important adjustment because some states are likely to trigger off of their EB periods in the near future despite high, sustained—but not increasing—unemployment rates.

States implement the lookback changes individually by amending their state UC laws. These state law changes must be written in such a way that if the two-year lookback is working and the state would have an active EB program, no action would be taken. But if a two-year lookback is not working as part of an EB trigger and the state is not triggered on to an EB period, then the state would be able to use a three-year lookback. This temporary option to use three-year EB trigger lookbacks expires the week ending on or before December 31, 2012. No state currently has an active EB program based upon this modification. Currently, only New York has an active EB program. (The TUR statistic for New York is 110% of the same period in the previous year.)

Temporary Federal Extensions of Unemployment Benefits: Congressional Intervention in Recessions

During some economic recessions, Congress has created federal temporary programs of extended unemployment compensation. Congress acted eight times—in 1958, 1961, 1971, 1974, 1982, 1991, 2002, and 2008—to establish these temporary programs of extended UC benefits. These programs extended the time an individual might claim UC benefits (ranging from an additional 6 to 63 weeks) and had expiration dates. Some extensions took into account state economic conditions; many temporary programs considered the state's total TUR or the state's IUR or both.

Historically, these programs started operation after the trough of a recession had passed (i.e., after the recession had officially ended). This is due to several reasons. One cause is that NBER often announces that a recession has begun three or more months after what is later determined to be the official start. Another cause to this lag in response time is that often the severity of the recession and its impact on unemployment levels does not become apparent until several quarters after the recession begins.

The 1958 and the 1961 programs were proposed and enacted after the trough of those recessions but before the unemployment rate had peaked. The 1971 program was enacted after the end of the recession in November 1970. Both the 1974 and 1982 programs also became effective toward the end of those recessions. The 1991 program was enacted eight months after the 1990-1991 recession trough but eight months before the unemployment rate peaked. Likewise, the 2002 program was enacted after the recession had ended but before the unemployment rate peaked. The current Emergency Unemployment Compensation (EUC08) program of 2008 was enacted seven months after the most recent recession began.[17]

---

[17] For a detailed description of the EUC08 program, see CRS Report RS22915, *Temporary Extension of Unemployment Benefits: Emergency Unemployment Compensation (EUC08)*, by Katelin P. Isaacs and Julie M. Whittaker.

Table A-1 located in the **Appendix** briefly summarizes these temporary programs[18] as well as the permanently authorized EB program. The 1982 Federal Supplemental Compensation (FSC) and 1991 Emergency Unemployment Compensation (EUC) programs had extremely complicated—and changing—benefit triggers. **Table A-2** and **Table A-3** (also located in the **Appendix**) provide detailed information on benefit triggers for those two temporary programs. **Table A-4** provides information on the current EUC08 program benefits and triggers.

Temporary Extended UC Benefits as Economic Stimulus

In the 110th Congress, congressional and popular debate examined the relative efficacy of expansion of UC benefits and duration compared with other potential economic stimuli. In his January 22, 2009, congressional testimony, the Director of the Congressional Budget Office (CBO) stated that increasing the value or duration of UC benefits may be one of the more effective economic stimulus plans.[19] This is because many of the unemployed are severely cash constrained and would be expected to rapidly spend any increase in benefits that they may receive and that the certainty of this behavior was very high.[20] Mark Zandi of Moody's Economy.com estimated multiplier effects for several different policy options, including extending unemployment benefits. Unemployment benefits had one of the highest estimated effects (1.64, where all proposed interventions ranged from 0.25 to 1.73).[21]

Others pointed out that increasing either the value or length of UC benefits may, however, discourage recipients from searching for work and from accepting less desirable jobs or that their spouses might forestall seeking additional work.[22] A rationale for making any extension in unemployment benefits temporary would be to mitigate disincentives to work, as the extension would expire once the economy improves and cyclical unemployment declines.

---

[18] The summary does not include P.L. 108-11, which created the special "TEUC-A" program. That temporary program was in response to the unemployment of airline workers resulting from the September 11, 2001, terrorist attacks, subsequent security measures, and the Iraq war. Signed into law on April 16, 2003, the program provided up to 39 weeks of extended benefits to individuals whose regular UC was based on qualifying employment with a certified air carrier, at a facility in an airport, or with a producer or supplier of products or services for an air carrier. The program had two tiers of benefits, known as TEUC-A and TEUC-AX and were authorized through the week ending before December 29, 2003.

[19] See CBO Testimony of Peter Orszag on Options for Responding to Short-Term Economic Weakness before the Committee on Finance United States Senate on January 22, 2008; http://www.cbo.gov/ftpdocs/89xx/doc8932/01-22-TestimonyEconStimulus.pdf.

[20] For another paper that takes this position, see the following: Douglas W. Elmendorf and Jason Furman, *If, When, How: A Primer on Fiscal Stimulus*, January 2008, available at http://www.brookings.edu/papers/2008/0110_fiscal_stimulus_elmendorf_furman.aspx.

[21] Mark Zandi, "Washington Throws the Economy a Rope," Dismal Scientist, Moody's Economy.com, January 22, 2009. The multiplier estimates the increase in total spending in the economy that would result from a dollar spent on a given policy option. Zandi does not explain how these multipliers were estimated, other than to say that they were calculated using his firm's macroeconomic model. Therefore, it is difficult to offer a thorough analysis of the estimates.

[22] For example, Karen Campbell and James Sherk, *Extended Unemployment Insurance-No Economic Stimulus*, Heritage Foundation, Center for Data Analysis Report #08-13, November 18, 2008. See also Martin Feldstein's testimony before the Committee on Finance United States on January 24, 2008, in which he stated that "[w]hile raising unemployment benefits or extending the duration of benefits beyond 26 weeks would help some individuals ... it would also create undesirable incentives for individuals to delay returning to work. That would lower earnings and total spending." Available at http://www.senate.gov/~finance/hearings/testimony/2008test/012408mftest.pdf.

Assessing the Labor Market: Determining When to Intervene

A variety of measures are typically used to assess the state of the labor market.[23] These measures may include statistics that are absolute measures, such as employment and unemployment levels, as well as relative measures, such as the insured unemployment rate and the total unemployment rate.

A vigorous debate on how to determine when the federal government should intervene by extending unemployment benefits has been active for decades. Generally, this debate has examined the efficacy of using the IUR or TUR as triggers for extending unemployment benefits. The debate also has examined whether the intervention should be at a national or state level. Recently, serious consideration of other measures of the labor market has become increasingly common. In particular, the increase in the number of unemployed from the previous year has emerged in several proposals as a new trigger for a nationwide extension of unemployment benefits.

Improving the UC System as an Automatic Stabilizer

The President's 2010 Budget proposal suggested changes to the UC system through the modification of the EB program in order to make the program more responsive to changing economic conditions.[24] While little information was provided as to the specifics of the legislation, the broad description echoes the recommendations of the Advisory Council on Unemployment Compensation first published in 1994.[25] The President's 2011, 2012, and 2013 Budget proposals did not have similar proposals.

Advisory Council on Unemployment Compensation's 1994 Findings and Recommendations for the Extended Benefit Program

The Advisory Council stated that the changing demographics of the workforce—coupled with state funding problems—had led to a decline in UC recipients. This had, in turn, caused the IUR to be a less reliable indicator of economic conditions at the state level and thus reduced the likelihood that the EB program would be active in the states during economic recessions. The Advisory Council also found that the temporary federal extensions of unemployment benefits have been "extremely inefficient" as they were neither well timed nor well targeted.

The Advisory Council generally supported that the EB program use a state TUR of 6.5% as an indicator of economic conditions meriting an active EB program.[26] They also suggested that any

---

[23] For a detailed explanation of the more common employment measures, see CRS Report RL32642, *Employment Statistics: Differences and Similarities in Job-based and Person-based Employment and Unemployment Estimates*, by Julie M. Whittaker.

[24] See the http://www.whitehouse.gov/omb/assets/fy2010_new_era/Department_of_Labor.pdf.

[25] Advisory Council on Unemployment Compensation, "1994 Findings and Recommendations: Extended Benefits," in *Collected Findings and Recommendations: 1994-1996. Reprinted from Annual Reports of the Advisory Council on Unemployment Compensation to the President and Congress* (Washington, DC, 1996).

[26] The Advisory Council also suggested that a modified IUR that also included those who had exhausted UC benefit in (continued...)

---

indicator not use historical comparisons or thresholds (e.g., 110% of previous year's level), which the Advisory Council labeled as "not helpful" since the threshold triggers caused the activation of the EB program to occur later and deactivate earlier than what the Advisory Council believed was appropriate.

The Advisory Council did not comment on the cost-sharing provisions of the current EB program.

Finally, the Advisory Council suggested raising the FUTA tax base from $7,000 to $8,500 in order to raise the additional funds needed by this suggested change. The President's 2012 and 2013 budget proposals included measures that would have increased the federal unemployment tax base to $15,000 while lowering the tax rate.

Using the Insured Unemployment Rate vs. Total Unemployment Rate

The Federal-State Extended Benefit Program, created by P.L. 91-373, originally assessed the labor market through both insured and "total" unemployment rates and included both national and state level triggers for extended UC benefits. The EB's federal trigger[27] was eliminated by the Omnibus Reconciliation Act of 1980 (P.L. 96-499). That act also required that the IUR measure not include those who had exhausted benefits or who were receiving EB. This effectively made the IUR statistic a less generous measure of unemployment.

Since the adoption of the permanent EB program in 1970, there has been considerable debate concerning the relative merits of the IUR versus the TUR as an EB trigger. The IUR is defined as the 13-week moving average of continuing regular UC claims divided by the average number of individuals in UC-covered employment. This means that the IUR itself is an output of the UC program.

Because the calculation of the IUR is based upon the number of individuals currently receiving UC benefits, each state's IUR depends on various noneconomic factors, including state eligibility rules and administrative practices. Thus, the IUR is not a precise reflection of the health of a state's economy.

In comparison, the TUR is defined as the number of all unemployed individuals actively seeking work divided by the size of the civilian labor force. The TUR represents a larger population than the IUR, because it counts as unemployed all those who are out of work and actively looking for work, on layoff, or waiting to start a new job within 30 days.

National, State, and Sub-State Triggers

A perennial question concerns the appropriate level at which to measure changes in unemployment. Generally this debate has centered on the EB program and whether the EB trigger should be based on national, regional, state or sub-state data. At the beginning of the most recent

---

(...continued)

the IUR calculation would be superior to the current IUR calculation.

[27] The federal trigger was an IUR of at least 4.5% for 3 consecutive months.

recession (but before the recession had been identified), the debate on the EB triggers was expanded to question what measure should be used if a new temporary extension of UC benefits were to be enacted. In particular, should Congress act as it has in the most recent recessions and create a nationwide extension of UC benefits with a nod to higher unemployment states through an additional "high-unemployment" trigger? Or would it be more appropriate and a better use of scarce resources to target only those states with current economic difficulties?

In the most recent recession, Congress first created a temporary program that did not target states based upon state unemployment rates (P.L. 110-252). Eventually, Congress expanded the temporary program and targeted much of the expansion of benefits to the unemployed in states that had higher levels of unemployment (first in P.L. 110-449 and then again in P.L. 111-92).

The argument in favor of a national trigger is that the definition of a recession is national in scope, and the federal government's interest in reversing an economic decline is national as well. However, recessions have often been primarily regional in impact. Thus, a national trigger can result in the payment of extended benefits to individuals in states that do not face unusually weak labor markets.

There have also been proposals to create triggers on either a regional or a sub-state level. The logic behind the sub-state or regional triggers is that they might improve the targeting of benefits because state boundaries are often of little relevance to the workings of labor markets. There can be considerable labor market differences between urban and rural areas within a state or among urban areas within a state. Furthermore, some labor markets are located in more than one state. A statewide trigger can deny benefits to areas facing severe labor market problems because other regions of the state are not facing the same conditions. There are a variety of arguments against regional and sub-state triggers. It would be difficult to define appropriate regional or sub-state boundaries, and it is unclear whether these newly defined regions would be any less arbitrary than current state boundaries. In addition, there are significant obstacles to be overcome in the financing and administration of an EB program on the basis of regional or sub-state areas, because the state has always been the operational unit for UC. There is also concern regarding the accuracy and availability of regional or sub-state data and the costs of data improvements that would be needed.[28]

Increases in Unemployment of at Least 1 Million Unemployed as Compared with the Same Month in the Previous Year

In the 110th Congress, debate moved away from using the IUR or TUR as a trigger for a national program. Serious consideration of other measures of the labor market has become increasingly common. In particular, the increase in the number of unemployed from the previous year emerged in several proposals for new triggers in a nationwide extension in unemployment benefits.

H.R. 4934, the Emergency Unemployment Compensation Act of 2008, was introduced on January 15, 2008. This bill would have extended UC benefits for up to 26 weeks when the

---

[28] The Advisory Council on Unemployment Compensation advised against the use of substate or regional data in determining the availability of extended benefits. Advisory Council on Unemployment Compensation, *Collected Findings and Recommendations: 1994-1996*, 1996, p. 5.

number of unemployed persons 16 years of age or older increased by at least 1 million individuals as compared with the same month of the previous year.

Table A-5, located in the **Appendix**, provides information on the timing of the recessions, changes in unemployment of at least 1 million compared with same month in the previous year, and federal enactment of the temporary extensions of benefits. During this period, the temporary extensions of unemployment benefits take effect between 4 and 14 months after the onset of the recession. The first changes in unemployment compared with the same month in the previous year of at least 1 million occur between 3 and 5 months after the onset of the recession. Therefore, if the "1 million" trigger had been in place in the past, the extension of UC benefits would have been triggered between 8 to 12 months earlier than actually occurred.

Figure 2 provides a graphical presentation of the information that was summarized in **Table A-4**, and it includes data on the unemployment rate.

Please note that **Figure 2** uses different numerical scales for changes in unemployment levels and for the unemployment rate. Because the correspondence between the two scales was determined by page size rather than by a particular reason, readers should not place any significance in the two lines crossing each other. The scale for the changes in unemployment levels compared with same month in the previous year is located on the left-hand y-axis. The scale for the unemployment rate is located on the right-hand y-axis.

Figure 2. Recessions, Changes in Unemployment Compared with the Same Month in Previous Year, Unemployment Rates, and Temporary Federal Benefit Availability, January 1979–July 2012

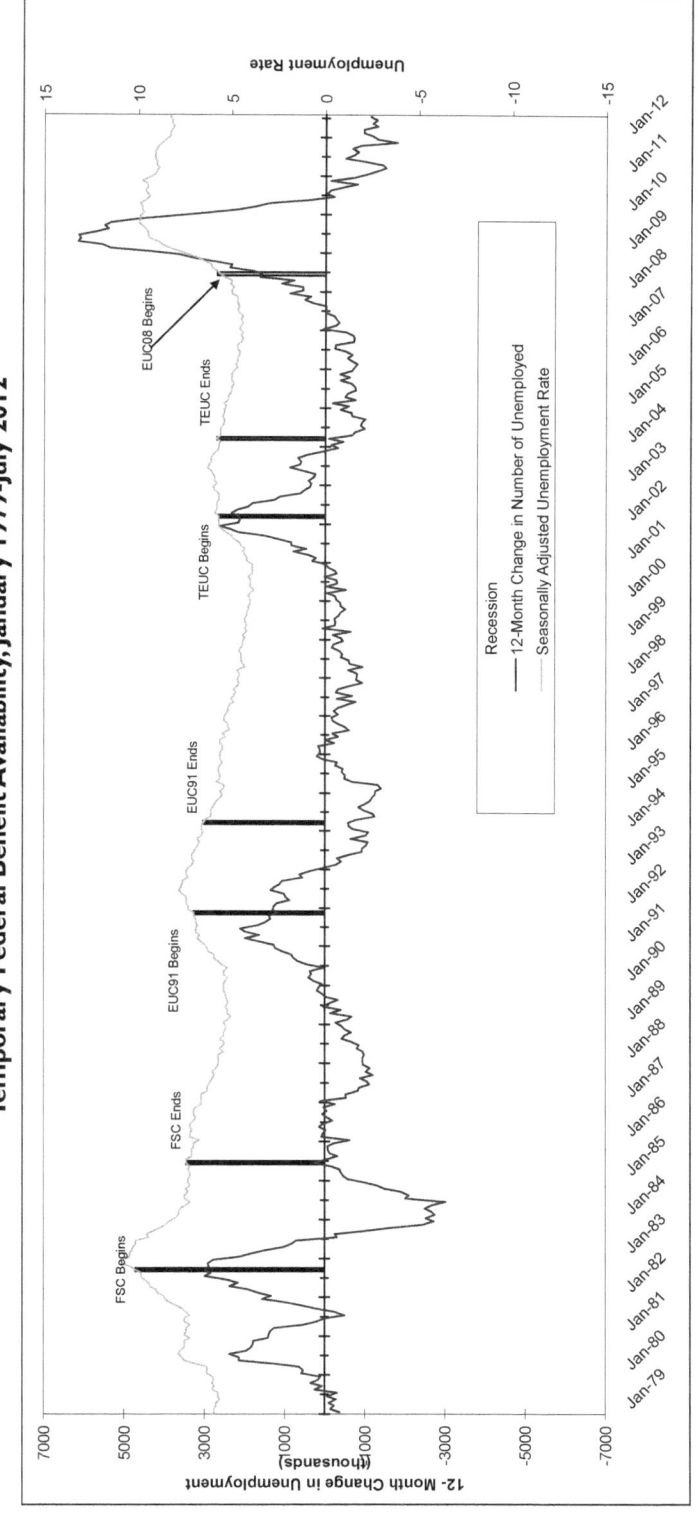

Source: CRS figure. Timing of recessions from National Bureau of Economic Research. Estimated changes in unemployment compared to same month in the previous year from the Current Population Survey data, Bureau of Labor Statistics.

Other Measures: Changes in UC Benefits Exhaustions and Changes in Long-Term Unemployment

Beyond the IUR, TUR, and changes in the total number of unemployed, several other measures of unemployment are often used in assessing the severity of employment conditions. These measures include the number of unemployed workers who exhaust UC benefits and the number of workers who have been unemployed for more than 26 weeks (the number of long-term unemployed).

Figure 3 shows the change in the number of exhaustion of UC benefits. **Figure 4** shows the change in the number of workers who have been unemployed for more than 26 weeks. Generally, both the changes in the numbers of exhaustees and the changes in the number of long-term unemployed peak after the end of a recession.

Figure 3. Recessions, Changes in Regular UC Benefit Exhaustions Compared with the Same Month in Previous Year, and Unemployment Rates, January 1979-July 2012

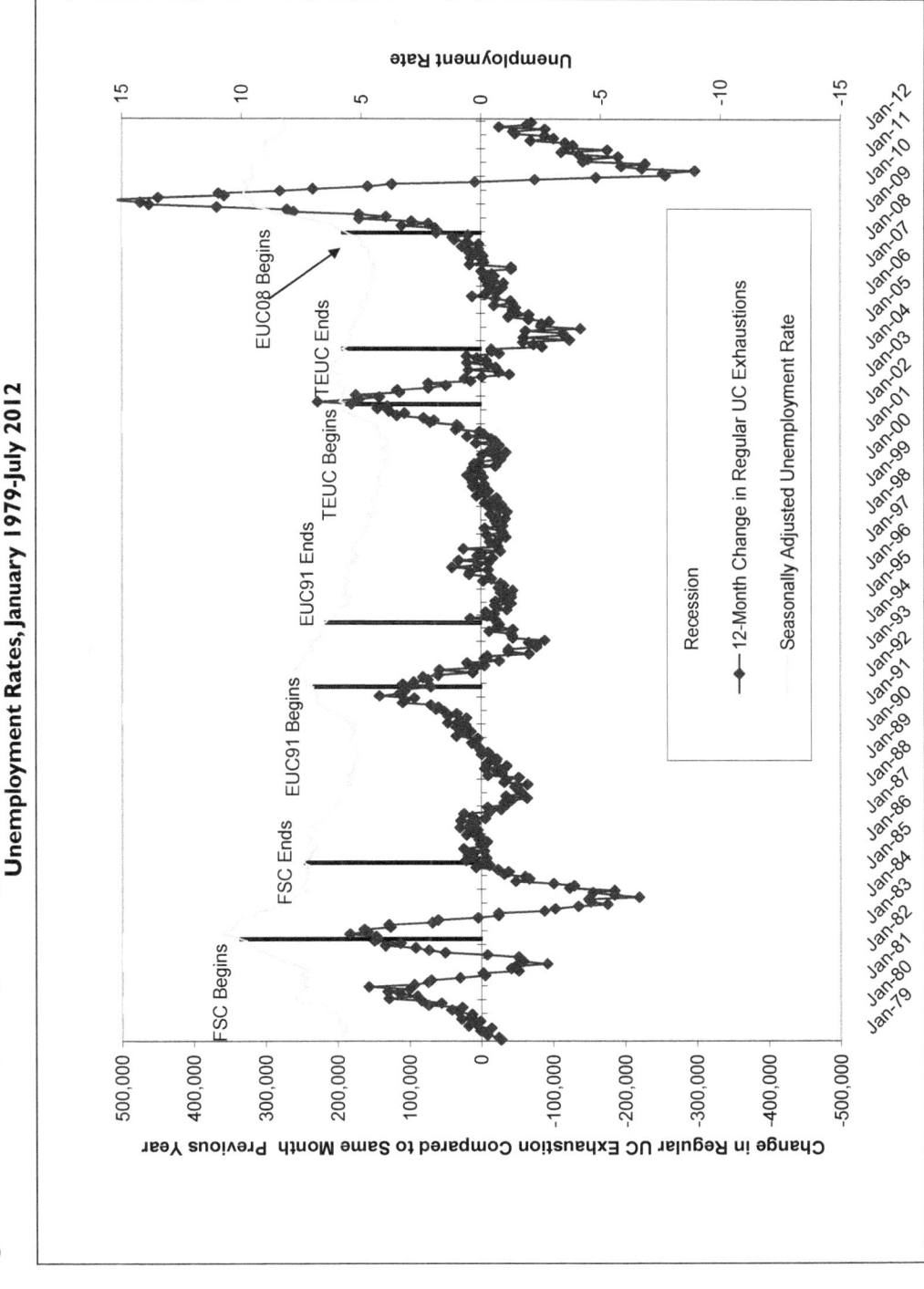

Source: CRS figure. Timing of recessions from National Bureau of Economic Research. Estimated changes in UC benefit exhaustion compared to same month in previous year from the Employment and Training Administration, Department of Labor. Unemployment rate from the Current Population Survey data, Bureau of Labor Statistics, Department of Labor.

Figure 4. Recessions, Changes in Long-Term Unemployment Compared with the Same Month in Previous Year, and Unemployment Rates, January 1979-July 2012

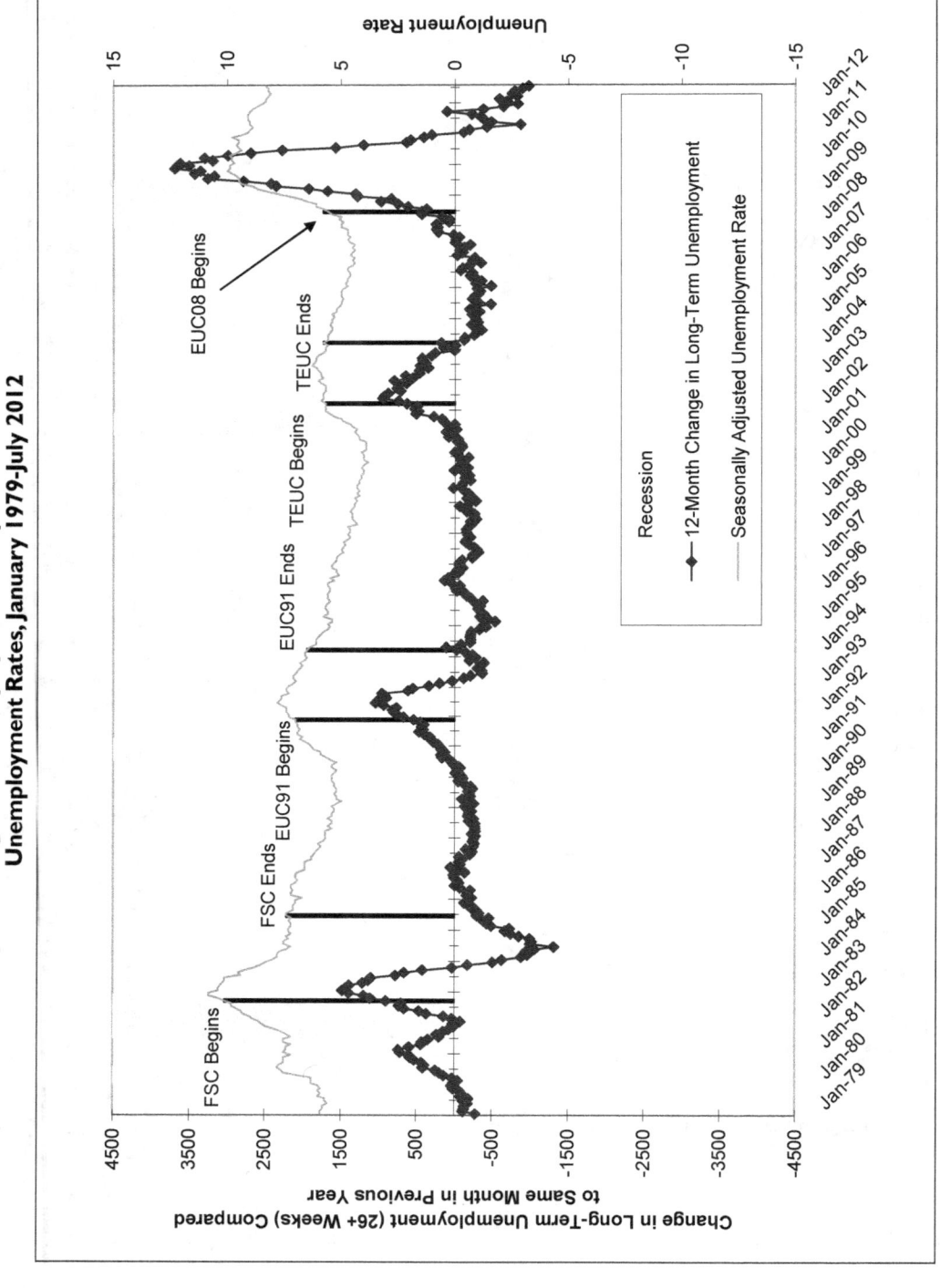

Source: CRS figure. Timing of recessions from National Bureau of Economic Research. Estimated changes in long-term unemployment compared with same month in previous year and unemployment rate from the Current Population Survey data, Bureau of Labor Statistics.

Congressional Interest in "Paying for Temporary Benefits"

Increases in Revenues or Decreases in Expenditures Related to Temporary Unemployment Benefit Legislation

Debate in the 111th Congress included substantial interest in whether benefit extension legislation should include measures to "pay for" the proposals and be subject to House and Senate PAYGO requirements or whether these extensions should be considered "emergency" measures and exempt from the PAYGO requirements.[29] With the exceptions of P.L. 110-449, P.L. 112-78, and P.L. 112-96, all laws that create, extend, or alter the EUC08 program have been treated as emergency expenditures or have been part of larger appropriation legislation. P.L. 110-449 expanded the EUC08 program from two to four tiers (from potential maximum duration of 33 weeks to 53 weeks) but did not extend the authorization of the program. The law included a 1.5-year extension of the FUTA surtax.

Historical comparisons with previous extensions of temporary unemployment benefits are difficult because of differing internal House and Senate PAYGO rules that have changed over time.[30] **Table A-6** in the **Appendix** lists all public laws that have created or altered these temporary unemployment benefit programs. The second column lists all decreases in federal expenditures or increases in federal tax revenues that are related to unemployment benefits within these laws. The last column includes explanatory notes that may put the laws into better context within this particular discussion.

The Congressional Research Service (CRS) identified 10 laws that included reduced expenditures or increased revenues related to temporary unemployment benefits.[31] Five laws increased the federal unemployment tax (FUTA) on employers. One law increased income tax on unemployment benefits received by individuals. Two laws increased the estimated withholding requirements for certain corporate income taxes. One law began to require interest payments from the states for federal loans to allow states to continue to provide regular UC benefits to their workers. P.L. 112-78 required new fees be paid when certain new federally guaranteed mortgages were issued. P.L. 112-96 did not declare the temporary benefits to be emergency spending and did include some offsets, including the auction of spectrum licenses and increased contributed to federal retirement plans. Some of the other laws did have reduced expenditures or increased revenues but are not included in this tally because (1) they were part of large appropriation bills and generally not subject to PAYGO rules or (2) CRS was unable to directly link these measures

---

[29] For example, see the text of consideration of S.Amdt. 3355. Senator Bunning stated "…As every struggling family knows, we cannot solve a debt problem by spending more. We must get our debt problems under control, and there is no better time than now. That is why I have been down here demanding that this bill be paid for. I support the programs in the bill we are discussing, and if the extension of those programs were paid for, I would gladly support the bill."

[30] See CRS Report R41157, *The Statutory Pay-As-You-Go Act of 2010: Summary and Legislative History*, by Bill Heniff Jr.

[31] In particular, either the increase was directly associated with unemployment benefits (e.g., increases in FUTA) or was an increase in revenue in a law where the only major increased expenditure was in altering the benefit structure or authorization time limit of the temporary unemployment benefit.

---

to any type of unemployment benefits. CRS did not attempt to identify whether these reductions in expenditures or increases in revenues fully offset the expected costs of the changes in expenditures on temporary unemployment benefits.

Congressional Interest in the 112ᵗʰ Congress: "Maximum Length of Total UI Benefits over Time"

Debate in the 112ᵗʰ Congress has included substantial interest in whether the total number of weeks of UI benefits available to workers is overly generous as compared with previous recessions. The EUC08 program has been amended 10 times by P.L. 110-449, P.L. 111-5, P.L. 111-92, P.L. 111-118, P.L. 111-144, P.L. 111-157, P.L. 111-205, P.L. 111-312, P.L. 112-78, and P.L. 112-96. This temporary unemployment insurance program provides additional weeks of unemployment benefits to certain workers who have exhausted their rights to regular UC benefits through a sequential array of four tiers, each of which is an individual entitlement.

On February 22, 2012, President Barack Obama signed P.L. 112-96, the Middle Class Tax Relief and Job Creation Act of 2012, into law. P.L. 112-96 extended the authorization for EUC08 through the week ending on or before January 2, 2013. It also substantially altered the structure of the program, creating three distinct EUC08 benefit time periods during the remainder of 2012: March through May 2012, June through August 2012, and September through December 2012. EUC08 tier duration and availability in states vary across each of these time periods. In addition, EUC08 tier requirements that establish particular unemployment rate thresholds in order that the state have an active tier II, tier III, and tier IV also change.

As of this report update, in states that have adopted the "TUR" EB trigger and have unemployment above 9%, up to 93 weeks of unemployment benefits may be available to unemployed workers (although only New York has an active EB program).

In comparison, the next highest maximum potential duration of unemployment benefits was during the Temporary Emergency Unemployment Compensation (TEUC) program in 2002 and 2003, when up to a total of 72 weeks for unemployment insurance (UC + EB + TEUC) were available in some states. **Table A-7** in the **Appendix** lists the total number of potential maximum available weeks of unemployment benefits available to the unemployed since 1935.

Appendix. Related Tables

Table A-1. Summary of Extended Unemployment Compensation Programs

Program	Public Law	Dates	Duration of Benefits	Trigger Mechanism	Financing Authority
Temporary Unemployment Compensation (TUC)	P.L. 85-441	[Reach back to 6/1957] 6/1958 to 6/1959	Lesser of 50% of the regular UC benefit entitlement or 13 weeks.	None.	Interest free loans to state accounts; if a state failed to repay loan by 1/1/63 the FUTA tax in the state was raised to repay the loan.
Temporary Extended Unemployment Compensation (TEUC)	P.L. 87-6	[Reach back to 06/1960] 04/1961 to 03/1962	Lesser of 50% of the regular UC benefit entitlement or 13 weeks.	None.	FUTA funds.
Federal-State Extended Benefits Act of 1970 (EB)	P.L. 91-373 (Amended several times. See also P.L. 96-499 and P.L. 97-35 below.)	Permanently Authorized	Lesser of 50% of the regular UC benefit entitlement or 13 weeks.	National: IUR: seasonally adjusted rate of at least 4.5% for 3 consecutive months State: IUR: at least 5% and 120% of corresponding period in prior 2 years	50% state SUTA funds. 50% federal FUTA funds.
Emergency Unemployment Compensation (Magnuson Act)	P.L. 92-224 and P.L. 92-329	1/1972 to 3/1973	Lesser of 50% of the regular UC benefit entitlement or 13 weeks.	National: IUR: seasonally adjusted rate of at least 4.5% State: IUR: adjusted for exhaustions of at least 4% and 120% of prior 2 years	Federal FUTA funds and general revenue.
Federal Supplemental Benefits (FSB)	P.L. 93-572, P.L. 94-12, P.L. 94-45, and P.L. 95-19	1/1975 to 1/1978	(Varied.) Provided up to 26 weeks of benefits.	National: IUR: seasonally adjusted rate of at least 4.5% State: IUR: at least 5% and 120% prior 2 years	Federal FUTA funds for benefits paid before 4/1977; federal general revenue for benefits paid on or after 4/1/1977.

Program	Public Law	Dates	Duration of Benefits	Trigger Mechanism	Financing Authority
Amendments to Federal-State Extended Benefits Act (EB)	P.L. 96-499, P.L. 97-35, and P.L. 102-318	Permanently Authorized	P.L. 96-499 tightened search and refusal of work requirements. P.L. 97-35 eliminated the national trigger, removed EB recipients from IUR calculations, and required that claimant worked at least 20 weeks recently. P.L. 102-318 added the state TUR option which allowed for up to 20 weeks of EB duration.	National EB trigger eliminated. State: IUR: at least 5% and 120% prior 13-week period in the previous 2 years; at state option IUR of at least 6.0%;. At state option TUR of at least 6.5% State TUR and 110% of prior 13-week period in either or both of two preceding years; an additional 7 weeks of EB if TUR is at least is 8% and 110% of either two preceding comparable periods.	50% state SUTA funds and 50% federal FUTA funds.
Federal Supplemental Compensation (FSC)	P.L. 97-248, P.L. 97-424, P.L. 98-21, P.L. 98-118, P.L. 98-135, and P.L. 99-15. (P.L. 99-272, some recipients in Pennsylvania.)	[Reach back to 6/1982] 9/1982 to 6/1985	Varied. See **Table A-2**.	Varied. See **Table A-2**.	Federal FUTA funds and general revenue.
Emergency Unemployment Compensation (EUC)	P.L. 102-164, P.L. 102-182, P.L. 102-244, P.L. 102-318, P.L. 103-6, and P.L. 103-152	[Reach back to 2/1991] 11/1991 to 4/1994	Varied. See **Table A-3**. [Note: Supersedes rather than supplements the EB program. Governors had the option of triggering "off" EB benefits.]	Introduced "average" IUR, a 13-week comparison measure. Varied. See **Table A-3**.	Federal FUTA funds for benefits paid before 7/5/1992 and after 10/2/1993; with certain exceptions, federal general revenue for benefits paid on or after 7/5/1992 but before 10/3/1993.

Program	Public Law	Dates	Duration of Benefits	Trigger Mechanism	Financing Authority
Temporary Extended Unemployment Compensation (TEUC, TEUC-X)	P.L. 107-147, P.L. 108-1, and P.L. 108-26	[Reach back to 3/2001] 3/2002 to 3/2004	TEUC: Up to 13 weeks. High unemployment states (TEUC-X); up to an additional 13 weeks.	TEUC was available nationally. TEUC-X was determined by state level: if the EB program was triggered on; or if the EB program would have been triggered on if section 203(d) of the Federal-State Unemployment Compensation Act of 1970 were amended to read IUR: at least 4% and 120% of the prior 2 years.	Federal FUTA funds.
Emergency Unemployment Compensation of 2008 (EUC08)	P.L. 110-252, P.L. 110-449, P.L. 111-5, P.L. 111-92, P.L. 111-118, P.L. 111-144, P.L. 111-157, P.L. 111-205, P.L. 111-312, P.L. 112-78, P.L. 112-96	[Reach back to 5/2007] 7/2008-3/2012 (scheduled end)	Varied. See **Table A-4**.	Tier I of EUC08 is nationally available. Depending on date, Tier II, Tier III & Tier IV EUC08 are determined at the state level. See **Table A-4** for details.	Federal FUTA funds. Benefits after February 17, 2009, were paid by general revenue.

Source: CRS.

Table A-2. Details: Federal Supplemental Compensation (FSC) Benefits

Public Law	Benefit Tiers	Dates in Effect (first claim date)
Tax Equity and Fiscal Responsibility Act (P.L. 97-248), signed 9/2/1982.	10 weeks: EB activated in state after 6/1/1982 8 weeks: EB inactive in state; IUR at least 3.5% 6 weeks: all other states.	9/12/1982-1/8/1983.
Surface Transportation Act of 1982 (P.L. 97-424), signed 1/6/1983.	16 weeks: IUR of 6% or higher 14 weeks: EB activated on or after 6/1/1983 but IUR below 6% 12 weeks: IUR at least 4.5% 10 weeks: IUR at least 3.5% but less than 4.5% 8 weeks: all other states	1/9/1983-3/31/1983.
Social Security Amendments of 1983 (P.L. 98-21), signed 4/20/1983.	*First FSC payments on 4/1/1983 or later:* 14 weeks: IUR of 6% or higher 12 weeks: IUR of at least 5% but less than 6% 10 weeks: IUR of at least 4% but less than 5% 8 weeks: All other states Additional entitlements for FSC recipients before 4/1/1983 10 weeks: IUR at least 6% 8 weeks: IUR at least 4% but less than 6% 6 weeks: all other states	4/1/1983-10/18/1983.
Federal Supplemental Compensation Amendments of 1983 (P.L. 98-135), signed 10/24/1983.	*FSC first payments on 10/19/1983 or later:* 14 weeks: IUR of 6% or higher 12 weeks: IUR of at least 5% but less than 6% 10 weeks: IUR of at least 4% but less than 5% 8 weeks: all other states *Additional entitlements for FSC recipients after 3/31/1983 but before 10/19/1983* 5 weeks: if all remaining benefits are for weeks before 10/19/1983 4 weeks: IUR of at least 5% 2 weeks: all other states	10/19/1983-3/31/1985. (No benefits past 6/1985).

Source: CRS.

Table A-3. Details: Emergency Unemployment Compensation (EUC) Benefits of 1991

Public Law	Benefit Tiers	Dates in Effect (first claim date)
Emergency Unemployment Compensation Act (P.L. 102-164), signed 11/15/1991.	20 weeks: States with TUR of 9.5% or higher or IUR of 5% or higher. 13 weeks: States with IUR of 4% or higher or IUR of 2.5% or higher and UC exhaustion rate of 29% or higher. 6 weeks: All other states.	Superseded by P.L. 102-182.
Termination of Application of Title IV of the Trade Act of 1974 to Czechoslovakia and Hungary (P.L. 102-182), signed 12/4/1991; and Emergency Unemployment Benefits Extension (P.L. 102-244), signed 2/7/1992.	*Claims filed before 6/14/1992* 33 weeks: States with TUR of 9% or higher or IUR of 5% or higher. 26 weeks: All other states. *Claims filed on or after 6/14/1992* 20 weeks: States with TUR of 9% or higher or IUR of 5% or higher. 13 weeks: All other states. [Note: P.L. 102-182 authorized benefit periods of 20 and 13 weeks; P.L. 102-244 authorized an additional 13 weeks for each tier.]	11/17/1991-7/3/1992.
Unemployment Compensation Amendments of 1992 (P.L. 102-318), signed 7/3/1992.	26 weeks: States with TUR of 9% or higher or IUR of 5% or higher 20 weeks: All other states. [Note: If national TUR fell below 7.0% benefits were to be phased down. This condition was not met.]	6/14/1992-3/6/1993.
Emergency Unemployment Compensation Amendments of 1993 (P.L. 103-6), signed 3/4/1993.	*Claims filed before 9/12/1993* 26 weeks: states with TUR of 9% or higher or IUR of 5% or higher 20 weeks: all other states *Claims filed on or after 9/12/1993* (triggered by national TUR falling below 7% for 2 consecutive months) 15 weeks: States with TUR of 9% or higher or IUR of 5% or higher. 10 weeks: All other states.	3/7/1993-10/2/1993.
Unemployment Compensation Amendments of 1993 (P.L. 103-152), signed 11/25/1993	13 weeks: States with TUR of 9% or higher or IUR of 5% or higher. 7 weeks: All other states. [Note: This law also made permanent changes to the EB program to make its benefits more widely available after the expiration of EUC.]	10/3/1993-2/5/1994 (No benefits past 4/30/1994)

Source: CRS.

Table A-4. Details: Emergency Unemployment Compensation (EUC08) Benefits of 2008

Public Law	Benefit Tiers and Availability	Dates in Effect and Financing
Supplemental Appropriations Act of 2008, Title IV Emergency Unemployment Compensation (P.L. 110-252), signed June 30, 2008	13 weeks (all states)	7/6/2008-3/28/2009 (No benefits past 7/4/2009) Funded by federal Emergency Unemployment Compensation Account (EUCA) funds within Unemployment Trust Fund (UTF).
Unemployment Compensation Extension Act of 2008 (P.L. 110-449), signed November 21, 2008	Tier I: 20 weeks (all states) Tier II: 13 additional weeks (33 weeks total) if state total unemployment rate (TUR) is 6% or higher or insured unemployment rate (IUR) is 4% or higher.	11/23/2008-3/28/2009 (No benefits past 8/29/2009) Funded by federal EUCA funds within UTF.
American Recovery and Reinvestment Act of 2009 (P.L. 111-5), signed February 17, 2009	Same as above. [Act included several other interventions that augmented UC benefits: the Federal Additional Compensation (FAC) benefit of $25/week; at state option, EB benefit year could be calculated based upon exhausting EUC08 benefits; 100% federal financing of EB program; and the first $2,400 of unemployment benefits were excluded from income tax in 2009.]	2/22/2009-12/26/2009 (No benefits past 6/5/2010) Funded by general fund of the Treasury. (Additionally, the FAC program is funded by the general fund of the Treasury. The 100% financing of the EB program is funded by the EUCA funds within the UTF.)
Worker, Homeowner, and Business Assistance Act of 2009 (P.L. 111-92), signed November 6, 2009	Tier I: 20 weeks (all states) Tier II: 14 additional weeks (34 weeks total, all states) Tier III: 13 additional weeks if state TUR is 6% or higher or IUR is 4% or higher (47 weeks total) Tier IV: 6 additional weeks if state TUR is 8.5% or higher or IUR is 6% or higher (53 weeks total) [Act included 1.5 year extension of the Federal Unemployment Tax Act (FUTA) surtax.]	11/8/2009-12/26/2009 (No benefits past 6/5/2010) Funded by general fund of the Treasury. Extended FUTA surtax through June 2011. The estimated revenues collected from FUTA surtax provision were $2.578 billion and offset the estimated direct spending costs for unemployment insurance provisions of $2.42 billion.
Department of Defense Appropriations Act, 2010 (P.L. 111-118), signed December 19, 2009	Same as above.	12/27/2009-2/27/2010 (No benefits past 7/31/2010) Funded by general fund of the Treasury.
Temporary Extension Act of 2010 (P.L. 111-144), signed March 2, 2010	Same as above.	2/28/2010-4/3/2010 (No benefits past 9/4/2010) Funded by general fund of the Treasury.

Public Law	Benefit Tiers and Availability	Dates in Effect and Financing
The Continuing Extension Act of 2010 (P.L. 111-157), signed April 15, 2010	Same as above.	4/4/2010 (retroactive)-5/29/2010 (No benefits past 11/6/2010) Funded by general fund of the Treasury.
The Unemployment Compensation Extension Act of 2010 (P.L. 111-205), signed July 22, 2010	Same as above. [Note this did not include an extension of the Federal Additional Compensation (FAC) benefit of $25/week for those receiving UC, EUC08, EB, Disaster Unemployment Assistance, or Trade Adjustment Assistance. The FAC expired on June 2, 2010.]	5/30/2010 (retroactive)-11/27/2010 (No benefits past 4/30/2011) Funded by general fund of the Treasury.
The Tax Relief, Unemployment Insurance Reauthorization, and Job Creation Act of 2010 (P.L. 111-312), signed December 17, 2010	Same as above.	11/28/2010 (retroactive)-12/31/2011 (No benefits past 6/9/2012) Funded by general fund of the Treasury.
The Temporary Payroll Tax Cut Continuation Act of 2011 (P.L. 112-78), signed December 23, 2011	Same as above.	1/1/2012-2/18/2012 (No benefits past 8/11/2012) Funded by general fund of the Treasury.
Middle Class Tax Relief and Job Creation Act of 2012 (P.L. 112-96), signed February 22, 2012	Tier I: 20 weeks (all states) Tier II: 14 additional weeks (34 weeks total, all states) Tier III: 13 additional weeks if state TUR is 6% or higher or IUR is 4% or higher (47 weeks total) Tier IV: 6 additional weeks if state TUR is 8.5% or higher or IUR is 6% or higher (53 weeks total); 16 weeks if no EB and all other conditions met (63 weeks total)	2/19/2012-5/26/2012 Funded by general fund of the Treasury.
Middle Class Tax Relief and Job Creation Act of 2012 (P.L. 112-96), signed February 22, 2012	Tier I: 20 weeks (all states) Tier II: 14 additional weeks if TUR is 6% or higher (34 weeks total, all states) Tier III: 13 additional weeks if state TUR is 7% or higher or IUR is 4% or higher (47 weeks total) Tier IV: 6 additional weeks if state TUR is 9.0% or higher or IUR is 6% or higher (53 weeks total)	5/27/2012-9/1/2012 Funded by general fund of the Treasury.

Public Law	Benefit Tiers and Availability	Dates in Effect and Financing
Middle Class Tax Relief and Job Creation Act of 2012 (P.L. 112-96), signed February 22, 2012	Tier I: 14 weeks (all states) Tier II: 14 additional weeks if TUR is 6% or higher (28 weeks total) Tier III: 9 additional weeks if state TUR is 7% or higher or IUR is 4% or higher (37 weeks total) Tier IV: 10 additional weeks if state TUR is 9.0% or higher or IUR is 6% (47 weeks total) Note: no phase down.	9/2/2012-12/29/2012 (No benefits past 12/29/2012) Funded by general fund of the Treasury.

Source: CRS.

Table A-5. Timing of Recessions, 12-Month Change of at Least One Million, and Extended Unemployment Benefits, 1990-2012

	1980 Recession		1981-1982 Recession		1990-1991 Recession		2001 Recession		2007 Recession	
	No Temporary Federal Extension	Months after Recession Begins	P.L. 97-248, FSC Benefits	Months after Recession Begins	P.L. 102-164, EUC Benefits	Months after Recession Begins	P.L. 107-147, TEUC Benefits	Months after Recession Begins	P.L. 110-252, EUC08 Benefits	Months after Recession Begins
Date began	January 1980	—	July 1981	—	July 1990	—	March 2001	—	December 2007	—
First 12-month increase in unemployment of at least 1 million	April 1980	3 months	November 1981	4 months	November 1990	4 months	August 2001	5 months	March 2008	3 months
Congress first enacts extension	None[a]	NA	August 1982	13 months	August 1991	13 months	February 2002	11 months	June 2008	6 months
Program becomes active	None	NA	September 1982	14 months	November 1991[b,c]	16 months	March 2002	12 months	July 2008	7 months
End recession	July 1980	6 months	November 1982	16 months	March 1991	8 months	November 2001	8 months	June 2009	18 Months
Last change of at least 1 million more unemployed	March 1981	14 months	April 1983	21 months	September 1992	17 months	September 2002	20 months	May 2010	17 Months
Authorization ended (does not include phase out)	NA	NA	March 1985	44 months	February 1994	42 months	January 2004	34 months	Scheduled: December 2012	Scheduled: 60 months

Source: CRS. Timing of recessions from National Bureau of Economic Research http://www.nber.org/cycles.html. Estimated increases of one million unemployed use data from the Current Population Survey, Bureau of Labor Statistics; http://www.bls.gov/data/home.htm.

a. The individual eligibility for the federal-state EB program was tightened by P.L. 96-499. The federal EB trigger was eliminated and the calculation of IUR was altered to be less generous by P.L. 97-35.

b. H.R. 3201 was passed on August 2, 1991; the President signed the bill (P.L. 102-107) but did not declare an emergency; thus, no benefits were available. Congress sent S. 1722 to the President who vetoed it on October 1, 1991. For a statement on the reasons for the veto, see http://www.presidency.ucsb.edu/ws/index.php?pid=20097.

c. Although P.L. 102-164 was signed into law on November 15, 1991, it was immediately superseded by two other laws: P.L. 102-182, signed 12/4/1991, and P.L. 102-244, signed February 7, 1992. P.L. 102-182 authorized benefit periods of 20 and 13 weeks depending on state economic conditions; P.L. 102-244 authorized an additional 13 weeks for each tier.

Table A-6. Funding Temporary Unemployment Programs

Public Law	Revenue Increases or Expenditure Decreases Related to Unemployment Benefits	Notes
Temporary Unemployment Compensation Act of 1958, (P.L. 85-441)	None.	This was a loan to the states for an additional 13 weeks of temporary state unemployment benefits. Loan had to be repaid.
Temporary Extended Unemployment Compensation Act of 1961, (P.L. 87-6)	Temporary Federal Unemployment Tax Act (FUTA) increase of 0.4% for 1962 and 0.25% for 1963.	
Emergency Unemployment Compensation Act of 1971, (P.L. 92-224)	None.	
[No title] (P.L. 92-329)	An increase in FUTA tax from 3.2% to 3.28% in 1973.	
Emergency Unemployment Compensation Act of 1974 (P.L. 93-572)	None.	
Tax Reduction Act (P.L. 94-12)	None.	Large bill with many tax reductions.
Emergency Compensation and Special Unemployment Assistance Extension Act of 1975 (P.L. 94-45), signed June 30, 1975.	None.	
Emergency Unemployment Compensation Act of 1977 (P.L. 95-19), signed April 12, 1977.	None.	
Tax Equity and Fiscal Responsibility Act of 1982 (P.L. 97-248)	Large bill. Offsets included: Increased FUTA wage base of individual annual earnings paid by employers from $6,000 to $7,000. Increased gross FUTA tax from 3.4% to 3.5% (employers in states with approved UI laws continued to receive 2.7% credit against FUTA tax so net tax is 0.8%); effective date: 1/1/1983. Increased gross FUTA tax from 3.5% to 6.2% (this included a permanent tax of 0.6% plus a an extension of a temporary 0.2% surtax that was to continue until all general revenue advances to EUCA were repaid; the offset for state employers increased to 5.4% so net FUTA tax remained at 0.8% until all general revenue advances to EUC have been rapid and then dropped to 0.6%); state experience rating schedules were required to have a maximum rate of at least 5.4%; effective date: 1/1/1985 but 5-year phase-in period. Reduced income thresholds limiting inclusion of state and federal UI benefits in adjusted gross income to $12,000 (from $20,000) for single taxpayers and to $18,000 (from $25,000) for married taxpayers filing jointly (waived estimated tax penalties for 1982 attributed to this change); effective for benefits paid on or after 1/1/1982.	
Surface Transportation Assistance Act of 1982 (P.L. 97-424)	Large bill. None.	Unable to identify UC specific offsets. However, bill revised the authorization of Highway appropriations which included increased fuel taxes.

Public Law	Revenue Increases or Expenditure Decreases Related to Unemployment Benefits	Notes
Social Security Amendments of 1983 (P.L. 98-21)	Required states to pay interest, when due, as a condition for all the State's employers to continue to receive offset credit against the FUTA tax and for the State to continue to receive grants for administration; effective date: 4/1/1983.	The "cap" on automatic FUTA credit reductions (available if certain solvency requirements are met) which was scheduled to expire at the end of CY 1987, was made permanent.
Federal Supplemental Compensation Extension of 1983 (P.L. 98-118)	None.	
Federal Supplemental Compensation Amendments of 1983 (P.L. 98-135)	None.	Study to examine how to prevent retirees and prisoners from receiving unemployment compensation.
[No title] (P.L. 99-15)	None.	
Emergency Unemployment Compensation Act of 1991 (P.L. 102-107)	None.	In order for EUC to be implemented, the President had to submit to Congress a separate declaration of a budget emergency that, in effect, would have allowed off-budget financing. Although the President signed the legislation into law, he did not issue the emergency declaration and thus the new program was inoperative
Emergency Unemployment Compensation Act of 1991 (P.L. 102-164)	Among other financing provisions: extension of 0.2% FUTA surtax for one additional year (through 1996); making estimated tax payment conform more closely to a taxpayers' liability; making permanent the tax refund offset program for collecting non-tax debts owed to the federal government; and improving the collection of guaranteed student loans in default.	Superseded by P.L. 102-182.
Termination of Application of Title IV of the Trade Act of 1974 to Czechoslovakia and Hungary (P.L. 102-182)	None.	
To increase the number of weeks for which benefits are payable under the Emergency Unemployment Compensation Act of 1991, and for other purposes (P.L. 102-244)	Amended Internal Revenue Code (IRC) provisions to provide for a temporary increase in the amount of certain corporate estimated tax payments, by setting the applicable percentage for such annualized payments at 95% of the tax liability for each of 1993 through 1996 (rather than 94% for 1993 and 1994, and 95% in 1995 and 1996).	
Unemployment Compensation Amendments of 1992 (P.L. 102-318)	Amended the IRC to extend by one year, through December 31, 1996, a phaseout of personal exemptions for certain high income taxpayers. Revised IRC requirements for corporate estimated tax payments. Required large corporations to base their estimated tax payments on an increased percentage of their current year tax liability as follows: (1) 97% for taxable years beginning after June 30, 1992, and before 1997 (rather than 95% or 93%, determined on an actual or annual basis); and (2) 91% for taxable years beginning in 1997 and thereafter (rather than 90%).	

Public Law	Revenue Increases or Expenditure Decreases Related to Unemployment Benefits	Notes
Emergency Unemployment Compensation Amendments of 1993 (P.L. 103-6)	None.	
Unemployment Compensation Amendments of 1993 (P.L. 103-152)	None.	
Job Creation and Worker Assistance Act of 2002 (P.L. 107-147)	None.	
[No title] (P.L. 108-1), signed January 8, 2003.	None.	
Unemployment Compensation Amendments of 2003 (P.L. 108-26)	None.	
Supplemental Appropriations Act of 2008, Title IV Emergency Unemployment Compensation (P.L. 110-252)	None.	
Unemployment Compensation Extension Act of 2008 (P.L. 110-449)	None.	
American Recovery and Reinvestment Act of 2009 (P.L. 111-5),	None.	
Worker, Homeowner, and Business Assistance Act of 2009 (P.L. 111-92)	Extended 0.2% FUTA surtax an additional 1.5 years (through June 2011).	
Department of Defense Appropriations Act 2010 (P.L. 111-118)	None.	Large bill, EUC08 funding was declared emergency spending.
The Temporary Extension Act of 2010 (P.L. 111-144)	None.	
The Continuing Extension Act of 2010 (P.L. 111-157)	None.	
The Unemployment Compensation Extension Act of 2010 (P.L. 111-205)	None.	
Tax Relief, Unemployment Insurance Reauthorization, and Job Creation Act of 2010 (P.L. 111-312)	None.	
The Temporary Payroll Tax Cut Continuation Act of 2011 (P.L. 112-78)	Required the Director of the Federal Housing Finance Agency (FHFA) to require each government-sponsored enterprise (GSE) (the Federal National Mortgage Association [Fannie Mae] and the Federal Home Loan Mortgage Corporation [Freddie Mac]) to charge a guarantee fee in connection with any guarantee of the timely payment of principal and interests on securities, notes, and other obligations based on or backed by mortgages on residential real properties designed principally for the occupancy of from one to four families.	

CRS-31

Public Law	Revenue Increases or Expenditure Decreases Related to Unemployment Benefits	Notes
Middle Class Tax Relief and Job Creation Act of 2012 (P.L. 112-96)	Large bill, EUC08 was not declared emergency spending. The bill included offsets; for example, the auction of spectrum licenses and increased federal retirement contributions.	

Source: CRS.

Notes: Some of these laws reduced expenditures or increased revenues but (1) they were part of large appropriation bills and generally not subject to PAYGO rules or (2) CRS was unable to directly link these measures to any type of unemployment benefits.

CRS did not attempt to identify whether these reductions in expenditures or increases in revenues fully offset the expected costs of the changes in expenditures on temporary unemployment benefits.

Table A-7. Potential Maximum Available Weeks of Unemployment Benefits, 1935-Present

Dates	Permanent Programs		Temporary Programs[a]		Total Weeks of Unemployment Benefits (Regular, Extended, and Temporary Benefits Programs)
	Regular Unemployment Benefits[a]	Extended Benefits (EB) Program[b]	Program Name	Duration of Program Benefits	
8/14/1935 to present (**first regular unemployment benefit check sent out 8/17/36**)	Up to 26 weeks				Up to 26 weeks (in the absence of temporary programs that provide additional weeks of benefits)
6/23/58 to 6/30/59 (reachback to 6/30/57)	Up to 26 weeks		*Temporary Unemployment Compensation (TUC)* (P.L. 85-441)	Up to 13 weeks	Up to 39 weeks
4/8/61 to 6/30/62 (reachback to 6/30/60)	Up to 26 weeks		*Temporary Extended Unemployment Compensation (TEUC)* (P.L. 87-6)	Up to 13 weeks	Up to 39 weeks

	Permanent Programs		Temporary Programs[a]		Total Weeks of Unemployment Benefits (Regular, Extended, and Temporary Benefits Programs)
Dates	Regular Unemployment Benefits[a]	Extended Benefits (EB) Program[b]	Program Name	Duration of Program Benefits	
10/10/1970 to 3/6/01 (P.L. 91-373 enacted 8/10/70; national-level trigger available after 1/1/1972; states given from 10/10/1970 to 1/1/1972 to include state-level EB trigger in state programs, although many states acted sooner)	Up to 26 weeks	EB Program Created. Up to 13 weeks of EB benefits if either national- or state-level triggers are reached[c]			Up to 39 weeks (in the absence of temporary programs that provide additional weeks of benefits)
1/30/72 to 3/31/73 (no reachback)	Up to 26 weeks	Up to 13 weeks of EB benefits if either national- or state-level triggers are reached[c]	Temporary Compensation (TC) (P.L. 92-224, P.L. 92-329)	Up to 13 weeks	Up to 52 weeks
1/1/75 to 2/1/78 (no reachback)	Up to 26 weeks	Up to 13 weeks of EB benefits if either national- or state-level triggers are reached[c]	Federal Supplemental Benefits (FSB) (P.L. 93-572, P.L. 94-12, P.L. 94-45, P.L. 95-19)	1/75-3/75 — Up to 13 weeks; 3/75-3/77 — Up to 26 weeks; 4/77-2/78 — Up to 13 weeks	Up to 52 weeks; Up to 65 weeks; Up to 52 weeks
9/12/82 to 6/30/85 (reachback to 6/1/82)	Up to 26 weeks	Up to 13 weeks of EB benefits if state-level triggers reached (EB national trigger was eliminated in 1981)[c]	Federal Supplemental Compensation (FSC) (P.L. 97-248, P.L. 97-424, P.L. 98-21, P.L. 98-118, P.L. 98-135, P.L. 99-15)	9/82-12/82 — Up to 10 weeks[e]; 1/83-3/83 — Up to 16 weeks[e]; 4/83-6/85 — Up to 14 weeks[e]	Up to 49 weeks; Up to 55 weeks; Up to 53 weeks
11/17/91 to 4/30/94 (reachback to 2/91)	Up to 26 weeks	Up to 13 weeks of EB benefits if state-level triggers reached (national trigger eliminated in 1981)[c]	Emergency Unemployment Compensation (EUC) (P.L. 102-164, P.L. 102-244, P.L. 102-318, P.L. 103-6, P.L. 103-152) Note: EUC benefits were reduced by any EB benefits received	11/91-2/92 — Up to 20 weeks[e]; 2/92-6/92 — Up to 33 weeks[e]; 6/92-9/93 — Up to 26 weeks[e]; 9/93-10/93 — Up to 15 weeks[e]; 10/93-4/94 — Up to 13 weeks[e]	Up to 46 weeks[e]; Up to 59 weeks[e]; Up to 52 weeks[e]; Up to 41 weeks[e]; Up to 39 weeks[e]

| Dates | Permanent Programs | | Temporary Programs[a] | | Total Weeks of Unemployment Benefits (Regular, Extended, and Temporary Benefits Programs) |
	Regular Unemployment Benefits[a]	Extended Benefits (EB) Program[b]	Program Name	Duration of Program Benefits	
3/7/93 to present	Up to 26 weeks	New, Optional TUR Trigger Provides up to 20 Weeks of EB Benefits (P.L. 102-318). In states without the optional TUR trigger, EB benefits remain capped at 13 weeks[d]			Up to 46 weeks in states that have adopted optional TUR trigger (in the absence of temporary programs providing additional weeks of benefits)
3/9/02 to 12/31/03 (reachback to 3/15/01)	Up to 26 weeks	Up to 20 weeks in states that have adopted optional TUR trigger,[d] otherwise up to 13 weeks (state may opt to trigger off EB if the state is on TEUC)	Temporary Extended Unemployment Compensation (TEUC) (P.L. 107-147, P.L. 108-1, P.L. 108-11, P.L. 108-26)[f]	Up to 26 weeks[e,f]	Up to 72 weeks
7/08 to present (reachback to 5/07)	Up to 26 weeks	Up to 20 weeks in states that have adopted optional TUR trigger[d,g,h] otherwise up to 13 weeks	Emergency Unemployment Compensation Act of 2008 (EUC08) (P.L. 110-252, P.L. 110-449, P.L. 111-5, P.L. 111-92, P.L. 111-118, P.L. 111-144, P.L. 111-157, P.L. 111-205, P.L. 111-312, P.L. 112-78, P.L. 112-96)	7/08-11/08 — Up to 13 weeks 11/08-11/09 — Up to 33 weeks[e] 11/09 -2/12 — Up to 53 weeks[e,h] 2/12-5/12 — Up to 63 weeks[e,h] 6/12-8/12 — Up to 53 weeks[e,h] 9/12-12/12 — Up to 47 weeks[e,h]	Up to 59 weeks Up to 79 weeks Up to 99 weeks[h] Up to 99 weeks[h] Up to 99 weeks[h,i] Up to 93 weeks[h]

Sources: This table was originally constructed by Alison Shelton. The information is from the U.S. Department of Labor, "Chronology of Federal Unemployment Compensation Laws" and "Special Extended Benefit Programs." Both documents are available at http://www.ows.doleta.gov/unemploy/laws.asp#FederalLegislation.

a. In 1940, only 1 state paid up to 26 weeks of regular unemployment benefits and 13 states paid no more than a maximum of 15 weeks of benefits. By 1950, 13 states paid up to 26 weeks of benefits. By 1960, 32 states paid up to 26 weeks of benefits and 9 states paid more than 26 weeks of benefits (these states generally paid around 30 weeks of benefits). During the 1990s, most states that had previously paid more than 26 weeks of benefits reduced the maximum number of available weeks to 26, as a result of state trust fund insolvency and the introduction of the Extended Benefits program in the 1970s. Source: July 9, 2009, e-mail from Jerry Hildebrand,

Chief of the Division of Legislation, Employment and Training Administration, U.S. Department of Labor. In 2011, several states enacted legislation to decrease the maximum number of weeks of regular state UC benefits. Until recently, all states paid at least up to 26 weeks of UC benefits to eligible, unemployed individuals with Montana paying up to 28 weeks of benefits and Massachusetts paying up to 30 weeks of benefits. In 2011, six states passed legislation to decrease their maximum UC benefit durations. Arkansas, Missouri, and South Carolina have made state UC law changes that are already in effect. Michigan, Illinois, and Florida legislated state law changes that will be effective in January 2012.

b. The permanent Extended Benefits program and certain temporary programs use unemployment rate thresholds, or "triggers," to determine whether the programs should be activated either at the state or national levels, depending on the program and the historical time period. The two unemployment rate triggers that have been used are the IUR and the TUR. The IUR is the number of unemployment insurance beneficiaries divided by the number of workers covered by unemployment insurance. The TUR is the number of unemployed workers (i.e., actively seeking work) divided by the total number of workers (employed and unemployed).

c. The Extended Benefits program initially had both national and state-level triggers. EB was activated nationwide twice: (1) from February 23, 1975 through July 2, 1977; and (2) from July 20, 1980 through January 24, 1981. During periods when EB was not available nationally, the EB state-level trigger requirements sometimes caused EB to be unavailable in states with persistently high unemployment. The state-level trigger requirements were therefore suspended seven times between October 1972 and December 1976. Revisions to the EB program in 1981 kept the maximum number of available weeks at 13 but eliminated the national-level trigger. The 1981 revisions also established more restrictive criteria for activating EB at the state level, through two provisions: (1) raising IUR thresholds that states need to reach to trigger onto EB; and (2) modifying the IUR calculation in a way that results in lower state IURs (specifically, eliminating EB claimants from the definition of unemployment insurance beneficiaries in the numerator of the IUR calculation). The 1981 changes to the EB program also added a second, optional, trigger for 13 weeks of benefits that states could adopt, effective for weeks after September 25, 1982.

d. The Unemployment Compensation Amendments of 1992 (P.L. 102-318) allowed states to make EB more widely available by adopting a third, optional trigger that would provide for 13 or 20 additional weeks of benefits depending on the state's TUR. Some, although not all, states cross the EB program's TUR trigger thresholds before crossing the program's IUR trigger. This is because of differences among states in unemployment insurance coverage (for example, the number of non-insured self-employed workers in the state) and also differences in states' eligibility rules and administrative practices that can limit the number of unemployment beneficiaries (the numerator in the IUR calculation, see footnote b).

e. The figure shown is the maximum number of benefit weeks that were available under the program during the given time period. Certain temporary programs, however, used benefit "tiers" to provide more benefit weeks to states with relatively higher unemployment rates than to states with relatively lower unemployment rates. For example, the FSC program provided up to five different tiers of benefit durations within a single time period. The FSC and TEUC programs, besides linking the number of benefit weeks to state unemployment rates, also linked the number of available benefit weeks in a state to whether or not the state's EB program had triggered on. The EUC08 program provided a single tier of benefits when it was first became effective in July 2008; this was expanded to four tiers of benefits in November 2008 and to four tiers of benefits in November 2009.

f. The TEUC program also provided an additional 13-26 weeks of benefits to certain unemployed airline employees.

g. P.L. 111-312 made technical changes to certain triggers in the EB program. P.L. 111-312 allows states to temporarily use lookback calculations based on three years of unemployment rate data (rather than the permanent law lookback of two years of data) as part of their mandatory IUR and optional TUR triggers if states would otherwise trigger off or not be on a period of EB benefits. This authorization for this option was extended by P.L. 112-78 and P.L. 112-96. The authorization now is set to expire on the week ending on or before December 31, 2012.

h. In 2011 and 2012, several states enacted legislation to decrease the maximum number of weeks of regular state UC benefits. Changes in UC benefit duration have consequences for the duration of federal unemployment benefits that may be available to unemployed workers. State UC benefit duration is an underlying factor in the calculation of duration for additional federal unemployment benefits. Thus, the reduction of the maximum duration of regular UC benefits reduces the number of weeks available to unemployed workers in the federal extended unemployment programs (including the Emergency Unemployment Compensation [EUC08] and EB). See CRS Report R41859, *Unemployment Insurance: Consequences of Changes in State Unemployment Compensation Laws*, by Katelin P. Isaacs, for a list of these states and estimates of the impact of the reductions on total potential weeks of unemployment insurance.

i. P.L. 112-96 capped the maximum number of weeks to not exceed 99.

Author Contact Information

Julie M. Whittaker
Specialist in Income Security
jwhittaker@crs.loc.gov, 7-2587

Katelin P. Isaacs
Analyst in Income Security
kisaacs@crs.loc.gov, 7-7355